PIONEERS IN THE SKY

by Alex Hall

Minneapolis, Minnesota

Credits
Images are courtesy of Shutterstock.com. With thanks to Getty Images, Thinkstock Photo, and iStockphoto. Recurring images – Elena Pimukova, Svetolk, Dancake. Cover – IgorZh, Cristian M Balate. 4–5 – Patrick Foto, MM2d. 12–13 – pzAxe. 20–21 – Everett Collection. 22–23 – Everett Collection. 24–25 – Amy Johnson Festival, Kingston upon Hull by Bernard Sharp, CC BY-SA 2.0 <https://creativecommons.org/licenses/by sa/2.0>, via Wikimedia Commons. 26–27 – John Mathew Smith & www.celebrity photos.com from Laurel Maryland, USA, CC BY-SA 2.0 <https://creativecommons.org/licenses/by-sa/2.0>, via Wikimedia Commons, Tim Evanson from Cleveland Heights, Ohio, USA, CC BY SA 2.0 <https://creativecommons.org/licenses/by-sa/2.0>, via Wikimedia Commons. 28–29 – Frank Romeo, givaga. 30 – VladyslaV Travel photo.

Bearport Publishing Company Product Development Team
Publisher: Jen Jenson; Director of Product Development: Spencer Brinker; Managing Editor: Allison Juda; Editor: Cole Nelson; Associate Editor: Naomi Reich; Associate Editor: Tiana Tran; Art Director: Colin O'Dea; Designer: Kim Jones; Designer: Kayla Eggert; Product Development Specialist: Owen Hamlin

Library of Congress Cataloging-in-Publication Data is available at www.loc.gov or upon request from the publisher.

ISBN: 979-8-89232-876-0 (hardcover)
ISBN: 979-8-89232-962-0 (paperback)
ISBN: 979-8-89232-906-4 (ebook)

© 2025 BookLife Publishing
This edition is published by arrangement with BookLife Publishing.

North American adaptations © 2025 Bearport Publishing Company. All rights reserved. No part of this publication may be reproduced in whole or in part, stored in any retrieval system, or transmitted in any form or by any means, electronic, mechanical, photocopying, recording, or otherwise, without written permission from the publisher.

For more information, write to Bearport Publishing, 5357 Penn Avenue South, Minneapolis, MN 55419.

CONTENTS

Your Journey in the Sky.................. 4
Jean-Pierre Blanchard.................. 6
Dr. Hugo Eckener 10
Orville and Wilbur Wright 12
Bessie Coleman....................... 16
Charles Lindbergh 18
Amelia Earhart 20
Amy Johnson 24
Bertrand Piccard and Brian Jones 26
Where Will a Journey in the Sky Take You? .. 30
Glossary............................. 31
Index................................ 32
Read More........................... 32
Learn More Online 32

YOUR JOURNEY IN THE SKY

This is your captain speaking. We are taking flight to follow some of the most amazing pioneers in the sky!

At one time, flying in the sky seemed impossible. Now, people fly every day.

Many brave adventurers took to the skies so that we could, too.

It is time to strap in and start our adventure. The sky is the limit!

JEAN-PIERRE BLANCHARD

1753–1809

First up is Jean-Pierre Blanchard. He was a French inventor who was interested in hot-air balloons.

Jean-Pierre created his own hot-air balloon and moved to England.

He wanted to be famous. Jean-Pierre decided to be the first person to fly across the **English Channel**.

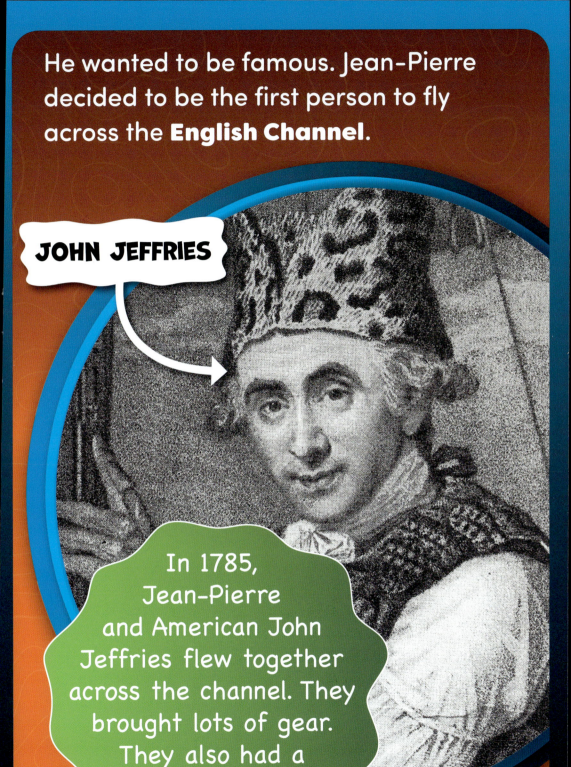

JOHN JEFFRIES

In 1785, Jean-Pierre and American John Jeffries flew together across the channel. They brought lots of gear. They also had a package to deliver.

Part of the way across, the balloon began to sink because of the heavy supplies. The men threw items overboard, including some of their clothes!

The pair landed safely in France and delivered the package. It was the first mail sent between countries by air.

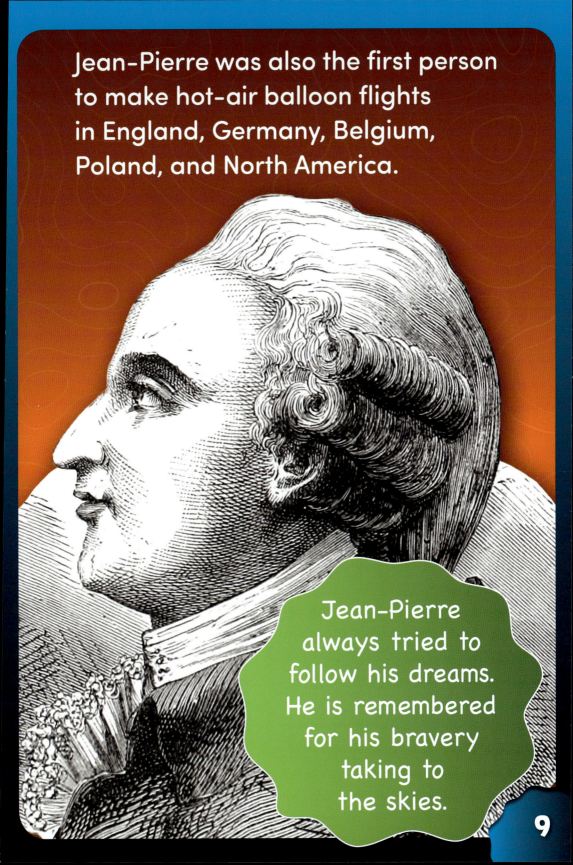

Jean-Pierre was also the first person to make hot-air balloon flights in England, Germany, Belgium, Poland, and North America.

Jean-Pierre always tried to follow his dreams. He is remembered for his bravery taking to the skies.

DR. HUGO ECKENER

1868–1954

Our next adventurer is Dr. Hugo Eckener. He was from Germany.

Hugo **commanded** huge floating airships called zeppelins. He set a record while in charge of an airship called the *Graf Zeppelin*.

In 1929, Hugo became the first person to fly an airship around the world. He set off from the United States.

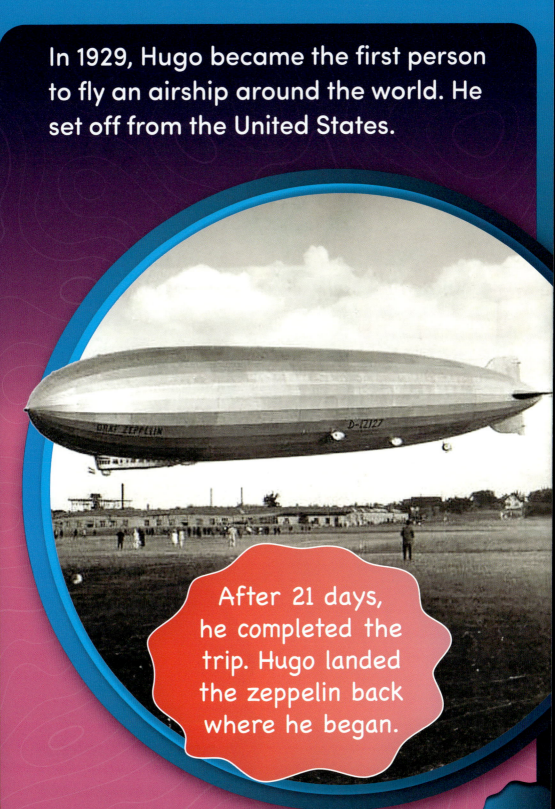

After 21 days, he completed the trip. Hugo landed the zeppelin back where he began.

Orville and Wilbur Wright

American brothers Orville and Wilbur Wright were inventors. Their creation flew them to fame.

ORVILLE WRIGHT

1871–1948

When the brothers were young, they played with flying toys. These toys started their interest in flight.

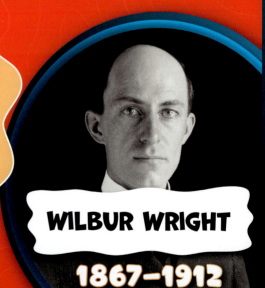

WILBUR WRIGHT

1867–1912

As the brothers got older, they began building their own flying machines.

They studied birds to come up with wings that could control their plane.

In 1903, the brothers completed the first controlled flight of a powered airplane. This flight lasted 12 seconds.

After more practice, they flew the plane for 59 seconds.

14

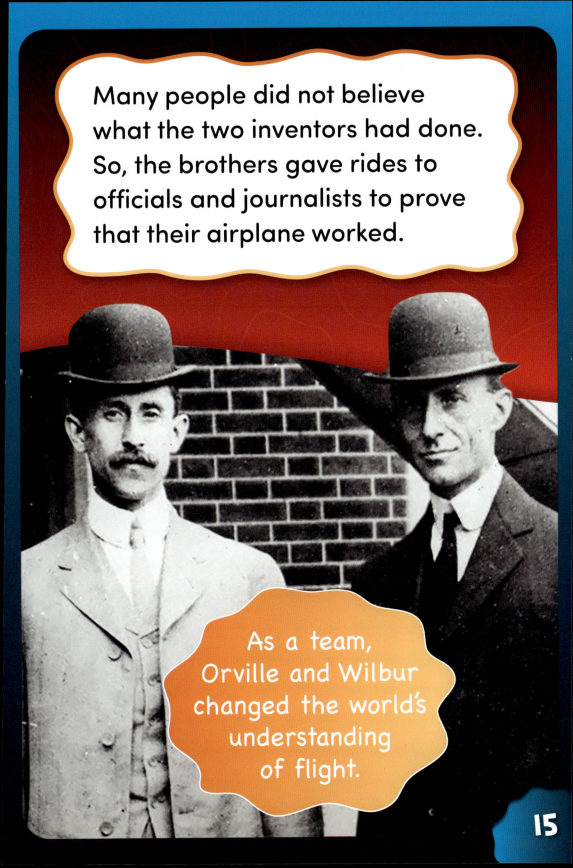

Many people did not believe what the two inventors had done. So, the brothers gave rides to officials and journalists to prove that their airplane worked.

As a team, Orville and Wilbur changed the world's understanding of flight.

BESSIE COLEMAN
1892–1926

Bessie Coleman wanted to be a pilot. However, American flight schools wouldn't take her because she was Black, Native American, and a woman.

So, Bessie learned to speak French and moved to France for flight school.

She became the first Black woman and the first Native American woman to get a pilot's **license.** She learned to do many risky airplane tricks.

Bessie returned to the United States and **encouraged** other women and people of color to become pilots.

17

CHARLES LINDBERGH

1902–1974

Charles Lindbergh began his adventure in New York.

Charles was a skilled pilot. He learned that someone was offering a prize to the first person to fly from New York City to Paris without stopping.

Many pilots tried and failed to complete this flight, but that did not stop Charles. In 1927, he set off. Charles landed in Paris about 34 hours later.

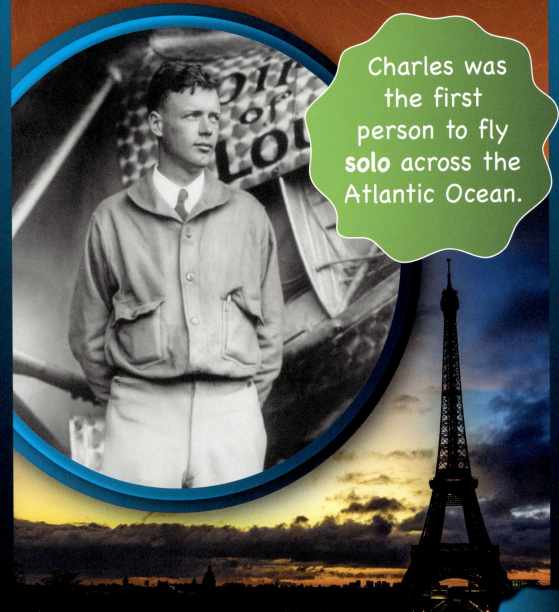

Charles was the first person to fly **solo** across the Atlantic Ocean.

AMELIA EARHART

1897–AROUND 1937

Get ready to fly with Amelia Earhart! She was an American pilot.

A few years after Charles flew across the Atlantic, Amelia decided she wanted to try, too.

She took flight from Canada and planned to land in France. However, bad weather and plane problems forced her to land on a farm in Northern Ireland.

Although her journey was difficult, Amelia made it. She became the first woman to fly solo across the Atlantic.

Amelia continued to set **aviation** records. She was the first woman to fly solo across the United States without stopping.

She was also the first person to fly solo from Hawaii to California.

Amelia wanted other women to fly. She helped start an **organization** for women who were pilots.

In 1937, Amelia tried to fly around the world. Sadly, she went missing during the trip. What happened to her is still a mystery today.

AMY JOHNSON

1903–1941

Amy Johnson was a British pilot. She began her adventure in England.

Amy wanted to fly to Australia. She used basic maps and drew lines across them to plan the fastest path.

24

She flew more than 11,000 miles (17,700 km). Amy faced very bad weather along the way, but she kept going.

Amy became the first woman to fly solo from England to Australia.

AMY'S PLANE

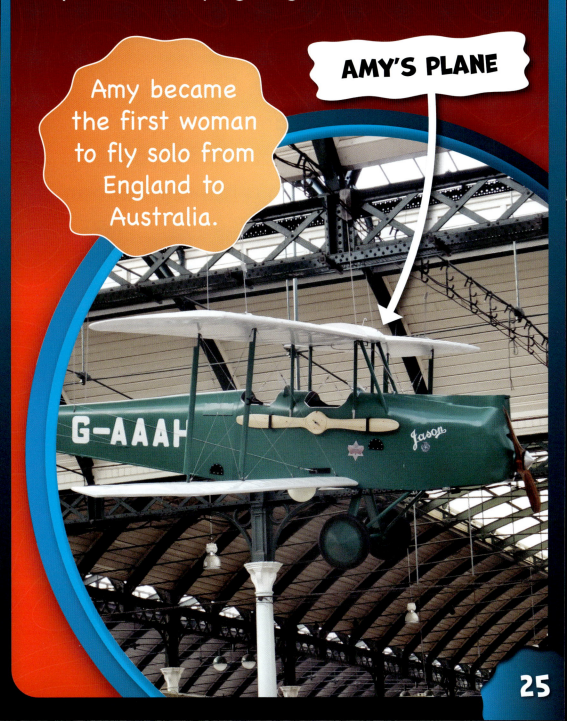

BERTRAND PICCARD AND BRIAN JONES

Our final flight is with Swiss pilot Bertrand Piccard and British pilot Brian Jones. They wanted to travel around the world in a hot-air balloon.

Many other people had tried, but they all failed.

BERTRAND PICCARD

BRIAN JONES

BORN 1958

BORN 1947

In 1999, Bertrand and Brian set off from the Swiss Alps. They flew south and traveled across Egypt first.

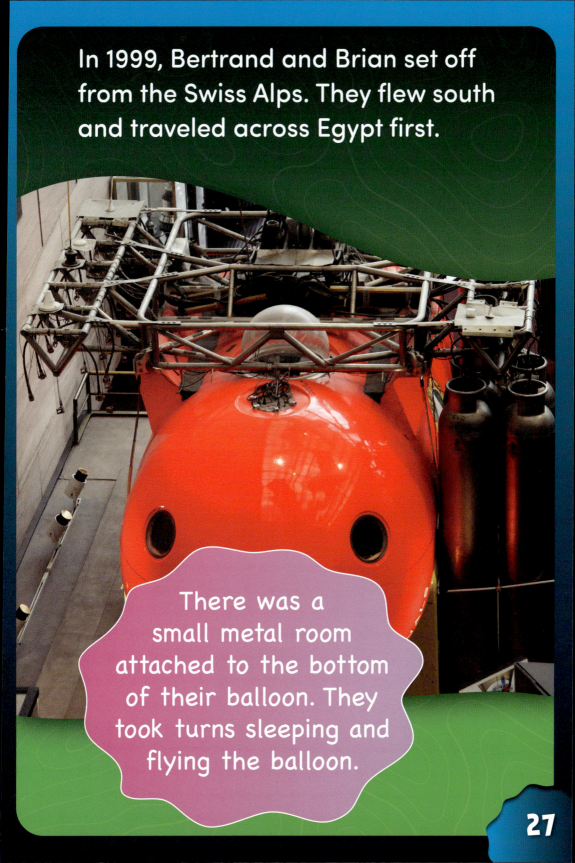

There was a small metal room attached to the bottom of their balloon. They took turns sleeping and flying the balloon.

Bertrand and Brian avoided many no-fly zones on their trip. These are places that are **dangerous** to fly through.

However, they got special permission to go through a no-fly zone over China. This helped speed up their journey across the Pacific Ocean.

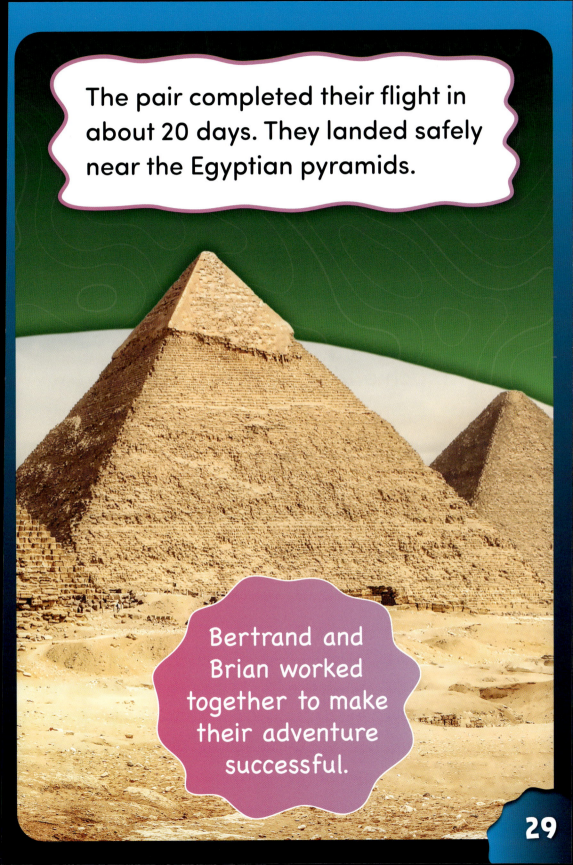

The pair completed their flight in about 20 days. They landed safely near the Egyptian pyramids.

Bertrand and Brian worked together to make their adventure successful.

WHERE WILL A JOURNEY IN THE SKY TAKE YOU?

Flying all around the world has been fun. There is still so much of the sky to explore!

Will you lead the next adventure in the sky? You could see so many cool things!

GLOSSARY

aviation the art and science of flying airplanes

commanded was in charge of

dangerous likely to cause harm

encouraged supported another person

English Channel the waterway between England and France

license a document that proves someone is allowed to do something

organization a group of people with a common interest or purpose

solo done alone or by one person

INDEX

airplanes 14–15, 17
Atlantic Ocean 19–21
hot-air balloons 6, 9, 26
inventors 6, 12, 15
maps 24
Pacific Ocean 28
pilot 16–20, 23–24, 26
pyramids 29
solo 19, 21–22, 25
toys 12
zeppelins 10–11

READ MORE

Cooke, Tim. *Amelia Earhart's Last Flight (That's Strange!).* Minneapolis: Lerner Publications, 2025.

Jones, Dale. *First Flights: Trips Through Sky and Space (Active Minds: Book of Firsts).* Chicago: Sequoia Kids Media, 2024.

LEARN MORE ONLINE

1. Go to **FactSurfer.com** or scan the QR code below.

2. Enter **"Pioneers in the Sky"** into the search box.

3. Click on the cover of this book to see a list of websites.